# SAFE HARBOR
## Begins @Home

Donald Hilliard, Jr.

*Safe Harbor Begins@Home*
by Donald Hilliard, Jr.

ISBN  1-58169-069-X
For Worldwide Distribution
Printed in the U.S.A.

Evergreen Press
P.O. Box 91011 • Mobile, AL 36691
800-367-8203
E-mail: info@evergreen777.com

# Table of Contents

# Dedication

IN GRATITUDE TO:

Robert Lee Crawford, *grandfather (age 89)*
Alease Crawford Hilliard Chapman, *mother*
The late Donald Hilliard, Sr., *father*
Sarah Ellen Slocumb Hilliard, *aunt*
The late Raymond Rollis Hilliard, *uncle*
The late Linda Lee Crawford Wright, *aunt*
The late Thelma Lorraine Hilliard, *special aunt*

———————————

Phyllis Denise Thompson Hilliard, *wife*
Leah, Charisma, and Destiny Hilliard, *daughters*
and to the generation that will follow...

God grant that the oil will continue to flow!

# Foreword

With more than 25 years of ministering to thousands of families, Dr. Hilliard is all too familiar with the challenges of raising God-fearing children in a society that contradicts God's Word. In *Safe Harbor Begins @Home,* Dr. Hilliard gives insightful, definitive solutions for making lasting changes not only for this generation, but for generations to come.

Unfortunately for many, home is a place of conflict, chaos, and confusion. A safe harbor is looked for outside of the home, regardless of the cost or consequences. In *Safe Harbor,* one cannot help but be awed by the value Dr. Hilliard places on home and family. Recognizing that God ordained the family as a sanctuary, Dr. Hilliard passionately, yet practically, offers biblically-based strategies on how to make the home a haven of safety. Promoting the biblical tenets contained in Deuteronomy 6:7 of teaching, talking, and spending time with your children, Dr. Hilliard gives practical solutions on how to create harmony in your home.

It is possible to begin again, to find a safe harbor. Let's go with Dr. Hilliard as he instructs us on how to make that safe harbor begin at home.

*Dr. Karen D. Wells*
*Clinical Psychologist*

# Introduction

*Safe Harbor Begins @Home* is the result of a series of messages that were prepared for the congregation of which I serve as the senior pastor. Over the years, I have noticed a downward spiral of the family unit. Absentee fathers, negligent mothers, and a broken-down community have given birth to a generation of angry, insolent, and bitter children. These children are often raised by television and movies that are filled with explicit sexuality and violence.

*Safe Harbor* is a call to parental responsibility in the family and the community. Each chapter outlines ways in which we can rebuild walls around our children and create a harbor that is safe and enriching. We are called to spend time and train our children in the way of the Lord. We can do this by talking with them, displaying tenderness, and reestablishing values and traditions.

As a father, I have done my best to make our home a safe harbor, where love and warmth are wrapped around each of our own children and other children who fill our home. My wife often teases me about making such a big deal out of holidays and vacations. I have found that these are often ways to fill our children with special memories that will help them throughout their lives.

For example, when our daughter left for college, we held a Holy Communion service around the kitchen counter. A small rock from the backyard was placed in her hands with the words, "Remember your foundation and where you have come from. We love you like a rock. Remember Christ is the rock of your salvation..." As she left our home, she took with her the strength of her parents and our unconditional love, joy, and confidence.

Around our home, I have lovingly planted three gardens in our backyard—one for each of our daughters. Pictures and poems that they have made hang in our family room. Each of our daughters was dedicated to the Lord in the same christening gown, which is framed and also hangs in our family room. My wife knows each of our daughters' favorite foods and prepares them with love and care.

All of these acts of love are contributing ingredients to making our home a safe harbor. The world can be a very cruel place, and home should be like an incubator whereby our children are connected, nourished, and cared for.

Perhaps much of what I do for my family is a result of what my parents tried to demonstrate for us as children. My childhood was filled with big dinners, visits to family members, parties, and tradition. It was important to my parents to make a big deal out of holidays. And they never made me feel that they were too busy to run us to a myriad of childhood activities. My mother was very active in the PTA and was a den mother for my cub scout troop. It was in that spirit that I wrote this book.

The core solution to the problems of violent crime,

teen pregnancy, drug and alcohol abuse, gangs, depression, suicide and a host of other items is contained in the family. We need to provide protection for our families and make our home a place of training from which our children can launch out into the world and fulfill God's wonderful plan for their lives. As we make each family and each home into a safe harbor, we are able to shine light in the midst of the darkness and sow hope and peace into our neighborhoods.

While there are universal issues that contribute to problems with our kids today, the solutions will involve more than a universal sweep of the hand or a catchall formula. Each family is different. Each parent will need to take this book and see how it fits them. Included are seven chapters of positive actions that parents can take in order to provide protection and training for their children. Each chapter is followed by helpful hints that can be used to make changes in your home. Be creative as you seek to follow these principles.

Above all, remember that God has ordained the family...His plan for it is wonderful. As we tap into that plan and learn to become responsible for our own harbor, we will experience His goodness in ways we never thought possible.

*Dr. Donald Hilliard, Jr.*
*Perth Amboy, NJ*

# Chapter I

# Walls of Protection—Build Them!

Picture your family living under a simple structure with a roof and four corner posts to support it—but having no walls. It offers you *some* protection, but probably looks more like the survival canopy of a castaway. Extreme temperatures and blowing rain or snow would still affect you considerably, not to mention the annoying insects and dangerous animals that would plague you.

Now, picture walls built around the structure. Yes, that's much better. You can choose what you want to allow into the building. Your family will be protected from the freezing temperatures and biting insects.

Whether it's an igloo, tent, apartment, or a modern home, man has typically surrounded himself with walls for protection.

Back in the days of the Old Testament, walls were also built around cities in order to provide people with protection from invading enemies. When a number of the Israelites returned home to Jerusalem from their exile in Babylon, they found the entire city in a mess. Their first project was to rebuild the temple, but because the city walls were broken down, their enemies freely moved among them as they worked and began to discourage them from completing their task. After awhile, spurred on by the Israelites' enemies, the king ordered work to stop. It wasn't until 25 years later that the temple was finished and dedicated, but there were still no walls of protection surrounding the city until about 75 years later when Nehemiah came on the scene.

Nehemiah's brother reported to him about the terrible state that Jerusalem was in—the walls were all broken down, and there was no safety for the people who had returned.

Does this sound familiar? Do you feel safe on the streets at any time of the day or night? Can you send your daughter to the store, or can your son play ball on the streets like you could when you were growing up? Crimes, drug dealing, and violence surround our communities on every side. All our families have been affected by it—whether directly, through assault or addiction, or indirectly, by anxiety and fears. It concerns me when little children of seven or eight years of age talk about having overwhelming problems. There shouldn't be serious problems for little ones of that age—they should be carefree. All they need to do is go to school, come home, play, do their homework, eat, sleep and enjoy one another. So why do these little ones have so many problems today? We must understand that children absorb so much from their parents. Today children are absorbing the trauma, pain, and tragedy that surround them.

## Place of Refuge

Nehemiah was the cupbearer to the king of Persia, and, as such, in a place of influence with him. Hearing about the predicament of Nehemiah's people, the King of Persia sent him to Jerusalem to help remedy the situation. It didn't take Nehemiah long before he saw the solution to Jerusalem's problem with their enemies. After thoroughly surveying the city, he called the people together and challenged them to begin rebuilding the walls around the city.

What does that mean in today's society? Should we react to the present situation and refuse to allow our children out the door? No, going to that extreme is not what we're talking about.

Let's look inside a typical home for a minute. Picture Nehemiah visiting your house.

"What's that box in the corner that everyone has their eyes glued on?" he might ask.

"Oh, that," you answer. "That's just the T.V.—it's nothing special—everyone's had one for as long as I can remember."

"What's all that shouting about?" he asks.

"Oh, that's just a show where some home boys are taking the turf back from their rivals. Shandra, flip the channel and let's see what else's on. Here's something you might enjoy—a crazy sitcom. Yeah, the daddy looks like a dope most of the time; but hey, it's funny, and you have to admit, there's no violence in this one. Don't like that one, Nehemiah? Flip again, Shandra. Here's one you can't argue with—a reality show. Now, this is *real* life. I admit, they *are* shouting at each other, but what's so bad about that? Everyone does it. Attitude? Well...I guess the young girl should be dressed more carefully, and the son shouldn't glare at his father. Hey, I give up...what *do* you want to watch?"

Does that scenario seem realistic to you? What kind of walls have we opened up to our children? What attitudes are we condoning by allowing our children to watch whatever they like? On Saturday mornings, we shouldn't even let our young children watch the cartoon shows unsupervised—it's unbelievable the amount of violence and bad attitudes that they contain. No, we must be diligent at *all times*. Kids are so impressionable. Defense arguments in criminal cases have even been based on the fact that some juvenile (somebody's boy or girl) killed someone else's child because they were imitating what they had seen on the screen. Of course, that's no excuse, but even lawyers recognize how much the media can affect our kids.

In a safe harbor, parents take the time to monitor what their children watch on television, what they are doing on the Internet, what music they are listening to on the radio, and what movies they are going to see. God is calling all of us parents to become like Nehemiah and build walls of protection in our homes so they can once again become safe harbors—places of peace and rest where our children can grow up with wonderful memories. It is only there that we can nourish and protect our precious children from the onslaughts of the enemy. It is only there that we can train them for the battles of life. And it is only there that they will become the blessing that God intended them to be.

Why are safe harbors not a part of the majority of our homes today? For the answer to that question, let's look at the words of Malachi, a contemporary of Nehemiah's.

# Changing Their Hearts

At the close of the Old Testament, Malachi described the condition of the people who were living in the land. It was a time when the priests had become lax, when the tithes were neglected, and when their sacrifices were not offered according to the Law. Their economy was suffering too, so the rich oppressed the poor, and dishonesty became the key to business success. The major problem, however, was the breakdown and fragmentation of family life manifested in rampant divorce and adultery. Because there was irresponsibility at the altar, it produced irresponsibility in every other area of their lives. If we're not responsible with the things of God, then we will not be responsible with our families. One of the signs of knowing God intimately is having a right relationship with those in your family with whom you live every day.

Does the situation in Israel sound familiar? The Israelites' families needed to be set in order in the same way that ours do today. Where did God begin with them? He began with a major reconciliation within their families.

A pastor friend of mine was on a symposium and someone asked him, "What is the major problem confronting your church?" Without hesitation, he answered, "the absence of fathers."

The absence of fathers has caused such evil in all

communities—black, white, Latino, etc.—that we are all suffering as a result. It is against God's design to have so many unfathered children. It is against His plan that our children should be looking to the media for their role models and values.

Since we are in the same state today as they were in the days of Malachi, let's look at Malachi 3:16-18 to see what God said He would do to remedy the situation.

> *Then those who feared the LORD spoke to one another, And the LORD listened and heard them; So a book of remembrance was written before Him for those who fear the LORD and who meditate on His name. "They shall be Mine," says the LORD of hosts, "On the day that I make them My jewels. And I will spare them as a man spares his own son who serves him." Then you shall again discern between the righteous and the wicked, between one who serves God And one who does not serve Him.*

God said that He will give us discernment and show us the way to serve Him. Then He followed this thought with the subject closest to His heart—family reconciliation. He concludes the Old Testament with Malachi's prophetic word on the family. He points to the new day that will be coming, a day that would mean not only redemption for individuals, but for families as well.

*And he will turn the hearts of the fathers to the children, and the hearts of the children to their fathers* (Malachi 4:6).

## How to Build

Today, we have a fantastic opportunity to change the lives of the next generation. As we begin to filter out unwanted influences in our home, though, we must be careful to replace them with positive ones.

We will spend the next several chapters discussing seven *positive* actions we can take to provide a safe harbor at home and make it a place of training from which our children can launch out into the world to fulfill God's wonderful plan for their lives.

**HELPFUL HINTS**

Take the next 4-7 days to monitor what comes into your home via: 1) T.V. and radio, 2) music, 3) the Internet, and 4) visitors.

This is not the time to make corrections, but to take stock of the situation. Make a list of each area that poses a problem. Then get before the Lord for direction. Don't try to change everything at once, but start somewhere. Sit down with your family and talk about the need for walls of safety. Address one area and then work at it until you're happy with the results. Then move on to another area. Your family's habits didn't form in a week, so it will take much longer than that to form new ones!

*It takes time to teach your children to pray and help them learn manners. It takes time to teach your children to love others and realize that the whole world does not revolve around them. It takes time to teach them respect. Whatever they spend the most time doing will be the greatest influence in their lives.*

# Chapter II

# Time—Spend It!

Let's look again at Nehemiah. When Nehemiah first heard the news that those who had returned to Jerusalem were in great trouble and disgrace, he sat down and wept. For some days, he spent *time* getting God's perspective on the situation before he took any action.

> So it was, when I heard these words, that I sat down and wept, and mourned for many days; I was fasting and praying before the God of heaven (Nehemiah 1:4).

Time. We need to spend time investing in the next generation in order to provide our children with a safe harbor. As Nehemiah did, let us, too, begin by surveying the situation. What is really happening in our homes? Are we permitting our children to be regularly exposed to things that do not contribute to their well being? What are they watching on television? Where are they going? What are they doing? And, on the other hand, what are *you* doing? What are *your* attitudes like?

When Nehemiah considered the situation in Jerusalem, he came to a place of repentance.

> *Please let Your ear be attentive and Your eyes open, that You may hear the prayer of Your servant which I pray before You now, day and night, for the children of Israel Your servants, and confess the sins of the children of Israel which we have sinned against You. Both my father's house and I have sinned. We have acted very corruptly against You, and have not kept the commandments, the statutes, nor the ordinances which You commanded Your servant Moses* (Nehemiah 1:6-7).

When we seek to make changes in our lives, we need to take time to find God's perspective. We need to take the time to talk to God about what we are doing and repent of any foolishness or sin on our part. Children learn so much by our example. What are we teaching them by what we are doing? We must first clean up our own mess before we can lead our families into a safe harbor. As it says in Matthew 7:5,

> *First remove the plank from your own eye, and then you will see clearly to remove the speck from your brother's eye.*

## Dealing With the Past

Some of our problems may stem from how we were raised as children. We may need to be delivered from the bitterness and anger we have toward our own parents who didn't spend enough time with us. Just because our childhood may have been crippled through a lack of good parenting does not mean our children have to experience the same thing. We can stop the vicious cycle of ineffective parenting by changing our ways of behaving with our children. Our God is a redemptive God.

We can choose to step aside from the past and forgive those who made mistakes with our upbringing. We must forgive and forget whatever negative things that were done to us. Then we need to let it go before we can move on to helping our own children.

## Time in the Harbor

After we have spent the time needed to get our life

right with God, we need to turn to our children and see how we can help them and how we can create a safe harbor for them.

A safe harbor is a home, first of all, where we gladly invest time in our children. My mother and father both worked every day, but somehow they found time to always have something good on the table for supper. Back then, dinner wasn't a bag from McDonald's. We had fried chicken, smothered pork chops, liver and onions, potatoes, and vegetables. Every day there were vegetables. If my father found that we had slipped ours into our napkin and put it in the garbage, he would go right to the stove and put some fresh ones on our plate. I resented having to eat brussel sprouts, but my father was right when he took the time to make me eat them. He knew that there were certain things that I needed in my body to help me to grow up strong.

When Mother worked late, Daddy spent time cooking for us. He did the shopping when Mother couldn't. But even though she worked all day, my mother still had the time and energy to take me to 4H, black student league, and student council meetings; band, track, and soccer practice (depending on the season); public youth debates and youth choir rehearsals. And she took my sister to Brownie meetings and dance practice. She drove us to all those meetings and never gave us the idea that we were an imposition. She always made us feel like we were worth the time she spent on us.

## Time—Spend It!

We create a safe harbor at home by making an investment of time in our children. Part of our decision to change is to ask the Lord to deliver us from being so self-absorbed and wanting to spend our time only on ourselves. We need grace to be the parents our children need us to be. We must put their needs above our own. Our children did not ask to come here.; they are a gift from God, and we must treat them as such.

If we say to them, "You get on my nerves," or, "I've been tired since the day you were born," how do you think that makes them feel? Even the people around Jesus wanted to shoo the children away. But what did Jesus say to them?

> *People were bringing little children to him in order that he might touch them; and the disciples spoke sternly to them. But when Jesus saw this, he was indignant and said to them, "Let the little children come to me; do not stop them; for it is to such as these that the kingdom of God belongs. Truly I tell you, whoever does not receive the kingdom of God as a little child will never enter it." And he took them up in his arms, laid his hands on them, and blessed them* (Mark 10:13-16).

Children are precious to the Lord. If you say to them, "Every time I turn around, you want something from me," what do you think that does to their self-esteem? Who are they supposed to get things from if they can't get them from their father or mother? Who should they ask? Do we want them to get it from people on the street? They are *supposed* to ask us. Of course, it wouldn't be good for us to give them everything they want, but if we don't *take the time* to listen to them and address their needs, we are making a big mistake.

> *But whoever causes one of these little ones who believe in Me to stumble, it would be better for him if a millstone were hung around his neck, and he were thrown into the sea* (Mark 9:42).

Children should not feel that they are aggravating our nerves and that they are the reason for all of our problems. If we say to them, "If it wasn't for you, I would have finished college," or "I could have had a fantastic job, but I became pregnant with you," we wreak havoc in their minds and devastate their hearts.

We must be thankful for our children and declare, as Hannah did about the long-awaited birth of her first son, Samuel, *"For this child I prayed."* We need to take the time to remind our children how much we appreciate the fact that they are a gift from God.

# A Better Way

Many of our children are growing up disconnected and disjointed because our homes are that way, but God is now trying to show us a better way. Hannah took the time she had with Samuel to mark him for God. It takes time to mark our children for God. It's more than throwing a few drops of oil on them at their dedication. It means *taking the time daily* to demonstrate our love for them.

We should not work all day and consistently have no energy left with which to invest time in our children. What does it profit us? We cannot allow ourselves to be so absorbed in our future and our careers that we do not have the time to be concerned about theirs.

If you have to work late, then spend extra time with them in the morning. Get up earlier than usual. We're talking about *balancing* your family life now. Break bread with them in the morning before they go to school. Or if you have to leave early for work, make sure that you come home and spend some time with them in the evening. If you have to be out of town for a trip, make sure they are the first ones that you tend to when you return. We must help our children to understand that they are our responsibility, and we are delighted with the opportunity to fulfill it.

In some situations, parenting seems to take more time than you have to give. Sometimes you may have to sacrifice and change your work schedule to be home when your children get home from school. Extreme? Yes, but there are times in your children's lives when that may be necessary in order to make the crucial difference.

One year I had to cancel or postpone five important preaching engagements. In some cases, my name was already published on the billboard, but I had to apologize and tell them I couldn't make it. Why? When I first accepted the engagements, I hadn't realized that some of them fell on the same day as significant activities or milestones of my children. It would have deeply hurt them if I had not attended. Years ago, I promised God that my children would never grow up pointing a finger at the church as a cause of their hurt or disappointment. My first obligation is to be their father. Before I am a pastor, a bishop, or a national speaker, I'm a daddy.

I remember when each one of my children was born, I was there with camera in hand. I cried as I held each child—their births were the greatest experiences of my natural life. I won't allow my children to grow up hating God because I missed their important school functions. Our children are with us for such a brief season. We should value them, spend time with them, and love them!

## Cutting Off the Crusts

What good memories will our children have about

family life? Among my memories, I am so thankful for tuna sandwiches. Let me explain: During some of my growing up years, my mother took in children because she needed the work and wanted to take care of my sister and I at the same time. Some of my most precious memories occurred in the fourth grade when I'd come home from school every day for lunch. My mother always had a sandwich prepared for me, and what touched me so much was the way she made it and served it. She cut the crusts off the bread because that was how I liked it, and carefully put the plate on the table alongside a napkin folded into a triangle. She always sat at the table and looked me in the face as we talked. I don't ever remember her putting lunch in front of me and walking away to do something else. For the 40 minutes I had at home for lunch, my mother sat with me and asked me about how my day was, and what was going on. I went back to school feeling special because Mama took so much time with me. That little tuna sandwich, prepared so lovingly, made me feel like I was in a safe place.

We don't know what some of our children are facing today; we all have heard of the terrible things that have happened in some of the schools. Sometimes our children will only begin to feel safe when they spend time in our presence.

Take time with your children. You may think, "I am just so tired, " but stop saying that in front of them and making them feel like it is all their fault. Grow up, drink a pot of coffee, take a nap, take 15 vitamins, but stop making your children feel like they are an imposition. They are a blessing from the Lord!

It takes time to teach your children to pray and to help them learn manners. It takes time to teach your children to love others and realize that the whole world does not revolve around them. It takes time to teach them respect. Whatever they spend the most time doing, whatever they are exposed to the most will be the greatest influence in their lives.

If we are going to create a safe harbor and give our children a heritage of holiness, we have to spend our time on them. Everyone is given the same amount of time each day, but what we do with it can determine the future of our children.

Time spent in the safe harbor will be time well spent.

## HELPFUL HINTS

When financially successful people are interviewed about what matters in life, they invariably say they regret not spending more time with their families. There is no substitute for time spent with children. Someone once said that you can tell how much you value or love someone by how willing you are to "waste" time with them. (It's not really wasted, of course!)

If you're a busy person, resolve today that you will reorder your life to make time for your family. Work first on increasing the *quantity* of time spent. Then work on improving its *quality*. Regardless of where we are in life, we are all given the same 168 hours each week to use or abuse. Set a goal to "tithe" 10% of your time each week to be with your family. If you do, you and your family will be blessed beyond measure!

*A good part of training children is creating order and discipline in their lives every day. Psychologists say that children who grow up eating dinner around the table with their family at least three times a week grow up more adjusted than children who don't.*

# Chapter III

# Training—Do It!

After Nehemiah arrived in Jerusalem with the king's letters of safe conduct and permission for procurement of building materials in his pocket, he took the time to thoroughly inspect the walls. He even went so far as to inspect some of it at night, so as to get the true picture of the task that lay before them.

But once his plan was formed, he didn't waste any time worrying about what had happened in the past to get the people to such a place. He gathered the people together and shared with them what God had told him to do. The people responded enthusiastically, and they immediately set to work.

23

We can't waste time with our families. We must begin the work *today* to restore the walls of protection so that we can begin the task of training our children for the life God has intended for them. Tomorrow will be too late.

## Positive Attitudes

*Protecting* them may involve saying "no" to some of the things they may want to do, but *training* them involves developing a myriad of positive attitudes and habits in them.

> *And, ye fathers, provoke not your children to wrath: but bring them up in the nurture and admonition of the Lord* (Ephesians 6:4).

Our children are supposed to be raised, nurtured, disciplined, and trained so that they will not be swept away by the temptations and obstacles they will encounter in life. The world tries to plant its own attitudes in them and subtly draw them away from God. Contemporary influences are affecting our children and clouding their judgment. Sadly, too few of us parents are taking the time to put into our children a real understanding of right and wrong. As a result, when these negative influences bombard them at school or in the neighborhood, they don't have enough inner strength or conviction with which to resist them.

Are we training our children for leadership in the days ahead, or are we letting them be swayed by the influences of this world? Are we training them to know God and be disciplined, or are we just giving them everything they desire without requiring anything of them? If we never deny them anything, we will raise children who are spoiled and have no character. We have to diligently and consistently work with our children to help them become responsible.

## An Example

Above all, we need to always keep in mind that we teach volumes by our example. We cannot say to them, "Do what I tell you to do, not what I am doing." The children will see the hypocrisy in that statement and will harden their hearts against learning what we are trying to teach them. When children hear their parents cursing each other or acting dishonorably or disrespectfully to one another, they will learn that behavior all too quickly. Parents may need to examine themselves to see where their children have learned this behavior.

*Do not be deceived, God is not mocked; for whatever a man sows, that he will also reap. For he who sows to his flesh will of the flesh reap corruption, but he who sows to the Spirit will of the Spirit reap everlasting life. And let us not grow weary while doing good, for in due season we shall reap if we do not lose heart* (Galatians 6:7-9).

We need to be open to hearing God's Word about His direction for our lives so that we can become examples of His ways to our children.

For example, my father taught me that if I made $100, I had to make sure that my parents would receive $15. When I went to college, I was surprised when they gave most of it back to me. They had saved it all those years. They weren't interested in using the money, but they were just trying to train me so that I would grow up to become responsible. I still give my widowed mother a check every month, not because she necessarily needs it, but because honoring her is my responsibility as a son. Recently, I was very blessed when our daughter did some babysitting work, and I found some of her money on my nightstand. I don't need her money, but I'm receiving it because I want to teach her character. We are trying to pass this tradition on to our children.

Many Christians were not raised with parents who followed God's ways. For example, there are entire families in which not one member has stayed married. By the power of God, generational curses can be rebuked, and a new pattern established. You cannot control what you came from, but you *can control* what comes from you. You cannot change where you came from, but you *can change* what comes from you.

We didn't choose our parents, but we don't have to follow their ways. That's why Paul said to the Colossian church, "Let the Word of Christ dwell in you richly" (Col. 3:16). Some of us need an entirely new road map so we can lead our families into healthy, wholesome living. We need a new agenda and a new set of rules and regulations that will help us create a safe harbor for our families.

We can make our old systems of relating and functioning in the home totally new. In other words, God will teach us how to be the parents we need to be. The motto for our families should be:

*But as for me and my house, we will serve the LORD* (Joshua 24:15).

## Order and Discipline

A major part of training children is creating order and discipline in their lives every day. Psychologists say that children who grow up eating dinner around the table with their family at least three times a week grow up better adjusted than children who don't. They say that children who have a permanent place at the table are more prone to earn greater academic achievements because of the order that is created in them. That means that Daddy always sits here, Momma sits there, baby brother sits between them, and so on. Every single day, everyone sits in the same seat. Dinner is scheduled to be around a certain time every day, and breakfast is served every morning. This is just one example of order.

Our generation is losing something when we ignore our children's need for order. We must help them learn self-discipline, or they will not be able to say "no" when temptations come their way. If they know, for instance, that they are required to get up by a certain time for breakfast, be home by supper time, and wash their hands before every meal, we have begun to make some boundaries in their lives. These may not seem important, but they are a structure that creates discipline in children.

Utilize mealtimes as an excellent learning time. Teach them how to set the table properly and wait until everyone is seated before beginning to say grace over their meals. Share a Scripture with them, discuss how it affects their lives, and help them memorize it. But above all, make mealtimes a time of sharing and caring with one another. Let them see discipline and order as positive things in their lives that will provide them with good memories.

After you have set up the rules and regulations, it is up to you to consistently make sure that they are enforced. It will take time and energy, but the rewards are worth it.

*Children, obey your parents in all things: for*

*this is well pleasing unto the Lord* (Colossians 3:20).

Children should know that that you mean what you say! You can't let them "get away with" something just because you are feeling tired one day. The more consistent you are, the more they will follow your rules and give you respect.

My father taught me respect for my elders and how to shake people's hands like a man and look them in the eye. They trained me to be respectful to others who are over me. However, when they thought I was being disrespected by an authority, they stood up against it. Some people have problems in their adult lives relating to authority because they never learned to have respect for the authority of their own parents.

As a boy, I could not sleep the morning away. I received directions such as, "Get up, walk the dog, feed the dog, wash something, clean something, read, and so on." Once my responsibilities were completed, I had the rest of the day to myself. But there was none of this going to the kitchen table to eat breakfast in my nightclothes—my father would have none of it. We had to get up, take a bath, and get dressed before we came down to the table. My father was a stickler for order. Now Mother, of course, was softer. We got away with more. The atmosphere was far more relaxed with her. They balanced each other out.

# Training for Serving

Children are born with the idea that the world revolves around them. In the beginning, we have to give them constant attention. Feeding time rolls around every few hours, and we quickly answer their every cry. But we can't allow them to continue to function as a newborn forever. Our job is to show them a better way. Our mission is to help them learn to put God and others first. Every time that you give them a dollar and tell them to put 10¢ in the offering plate, you are teaching them a lesson about giving their first fruits to the Lord. On Christmas morning, before you open one present, have them take turns reading the Christmas story about God's greatest gift to us. Then let them choose one of their own toys to give away to those who have nothing. You are teaching them to put others first.

We help them learn sacrifice when we take them to senior citizens' homes and visit with the elderly, or work in a soup kitchen for the needy. All of these activities help them keep their priorities right. But above all, we must teach them how to know God.

# Knowing God

Just as we need to get our lives right before God, so do our children. The underlying thing we always need to keep in mind for our kids is that in everything we do, we should be leading them to God. Our children need to have an understanding of who He is, and what He can do. They need to know His love, His mercy, and His power. We need to teach them the Bible so that it will come alive for them and be a rich part of their lives. We not only need to teach them to pray, but also to praise Him at their bedside. Teach them to thank Him for His protection and grace and for all the little things that are happening in their lives. Teach them to turn to Him with their problems, expecting and trusting in His love.

Training our children through order and discipline will help build a wall of protection in the lives of our children. It will create the safe harbor that they need in days such as these.

### HELPFUL HINTS

When it comes to training, make sure you are *consistent*. Before you set down a rule, make sure that you are willing to enforce it ALL THE TIME. After awhile, they will get the message and know that you will not change the rules on a whim, but are trying to *build* qualities of lasting value in them.

*Set them an example
by doing what is good and
showing integrity and soundness
of speech. When you sow good
things into your children, you
will be worthy of their trust
and can speak into their
lives with confidence. When
they trust you, they will
be anchored in a
safe harbor.*

# Chapter IV

# Trust—Deserve It!

After Nehemiah and the Israelites began to rebuild the wall in Jerusalem, they ran into opposition to the plan from their enemies.

Sanballat and Tobiah mocked the Jews and prophesied that nothing would come of their building. At this, Nehemiah prayed,

> *Hear, O our God, for we are despised; turn their reproach on their own heads, and give them as plunder to a land of captivity! Do not cover their iniquity, and do not let their sin be blotted out from before You; for they have provoked You*

*to anger before the builders. So we built the wall, and the entire wall was joined together up to half its height, for the people had a mind to work* (Nehemiah 4:4-6).

The people held together because of the trust they had in Nehemiah and erected the wall to half its original height in no time at all. But they didn't stop building at that point, they pressed on because of the confidence they had in Nehemiah.

When the going gets tough for our children, will they give up and give in to the temptations surrounding them? The answer to that question can be determined by the amount of trust they have in us as parents. Are we not just "talking the talk" but also "walking the walk"? Are our lives lined up with the Word of God?

God takes leadership very seriously. Do you play with the tithe by saying, "I'm going to give part of the tithe this week and the rest of the tithe next month because I am getting ready to go on vacation"? If God has your heart, He should also have your money. If God has your heart, He should also have your mind and your sexuality. All aspects of your life should be under His rule.

This so important because our children will follow our leadership. If we want them to have a close relationship with God, we need, first of all, to have one ourselves. They will follow us just as the people followed Nehemiah. They trusted him even though the Israelites' enemies were discouraging them at every turn .

## Anger Destroys Relationships

We need to be worthy of our children's trust. Are you making your home a happy home? If you try to hurt your spouse, you are really hurting your children. When you don't talk to one another because of some argument or begin to throw things around the house in anger, you are destroying your children. You are snatching away the safety and joy and peace that they should have. If you hardly ever smile, you are breeding a spirit of depression in your home. If you don't allow the joy of the Lord to flow from you, then anger will most likely take its place.

Anger is so destructive to our family life. The Scripture states,

*So then, my beloved brethren, let every man be swift to hear, slow to speak, slow to wrath; for the wrath of man does not produce the righteousness of God* (James 1:19-20).

Anger does not produce godly fruit. When we consistently react in anger toward our children, it can prevent our children from ever hearing their pastor. I received a letter from a woman years ago explaining why she had trouble responding to what I preached. She said, "Bishop, it was never because of you, it was because of my father."

Sometimes because of lack of attention on our part,

children may strike back in anger at us through disobedience or even breaking the law. If we don't deal with the problem at an early stage, they may progress in crime until they are sent to jail. But there is good news! The God who saved you, healed you, and raised you from your sick bed will help you learn a new way of behavior toward your children. You will see that spending your time, your talent, and your love on them will have a lasting, positive effect.

*But as for you, speak the things which are proper for sound doctrine: that the older men be sober, reverent, temperate, sound in faith, in love, in patience; the older women likewise, that they be reverent in behavior, not slanderers, not given to much wine, teachers of good things that they admonish the young women to love their husbands, to love their children* (Titus 2:1-4).

Many children don't rise up and call their parents blessed because of the type of lives they see their parents living before them. Children are so impressionable. We really need to take special care in our behavior. It's hard for a child to respect a parent when someone other than the spouse is in their parents' bed. When these little ones become teenagers, they will begin to follow the same path of looseness because they have not seen a a positive role model. It is difficult for a child to respect a parent who puts more emphasis on their own personal pleasure rather than their obligation as parents. The children have no one they can trust for proper direction in their lives. Before we can *teach* them the truth, we must *live* the truth!

## No Greater Call

The responsibility to nurture my children and to model for them a godly life sometimes seems overwhelming, but there is no greater call. And those who fulfill that call, who try to do the best they can by spending time with their children, by paying the bills, by disciplining them, and by praying with and for their children are parents who will receive the lifetime trust of their children.

For those of you no longer married to the father or mother of your children, stop tearing the other one down in front of them. If the truth be told, many of you were partly to blame for the separation or divorce. What your children need now is support and love from *both* their parents. Thank the other one for all they are doing to contribute to their children's lives. If you tear them down in front of your children, you will create distrust. Let go of the bitterness and pain so that you can develop trust in your children for you. Let God deal with your spouse. Trust Him to work it out, and as you trust the Lord, so, too, will your children.

In everything, set them an example by doing what is good, and showing integrity and soundness of speech so that no one will have anything evil to say of you. When you sow good things into your children, you will be worthy of their trust and be able to speak into their lives with confidence. When they trust you, they will be anchored in a safe harbor.

## HELPFUL HINTS

Begin by making changes in your own life. When they see you living out a principle, it will go a long way toward training them. For example, if you struggle with order and discipline, it will be difficult to teach it to your family. Spend some time working it out in your life and then begin to teach it to them. Perhaps you can make it a family project—something you can all work on together. They will have seen what a difference it has already made for you and not be as resistant to change in their lives.

*Both your daughters and
your sons need tenderness.
They need what I call "lap time."
Have them sit down by you
and let them know they
are a blessing. Say things
like, "From the moment God
sent you, you have been a
blessing to me. I just don't
know what I'd do
without you."*

# Chapter V

# Tenderness—Show It!

After Nehemiah and his people had closed the gaps in the wall, their enemies were still determined to overcome them. Until the wall was completely finished and the gates set in place, the Israelites had to spend their time either in guard duty or building. They were stationed by families, which meant that none of them could work and earn money to live, so the people were forced to borrow money from the nobles and officials.

The people began to cry out to Nehemiah for relief from their situation. Nehemiah surveyed the situation and realized that the nobles and officials were exacting usury from their own countrymen and so he said to them,

> *What you are doing is not good. Should you not walk in the fear of our God because of the reproach of the nations, our enemies? I also, with my brethren and my servants, am lending them money and grain. Please, let us stop this usury! Restore now to them, even this day, their lands, their vineyards, their olive groves, and their houses, also a hundredth of the money and the grain, the new wine and the oil, that you have charged them* (Nehemiah 5:9-11).

Nehemiah did not let the task of building the walls of Jerusalem prevent him from taking care of the needs of the people.

## Compassion and Mercy

No matter what we are involved in at work, and no matter what tasks are before us at home, our children should be confident that we will see to their needs. They need to know that we will take the time to consistently and correctly discipline them and not ignore the situation or, on the other hand, react to them out of anger.

Our children need to feel our compassion and mercy upon them despite what they may have done. Discipline cannot be effectively carried out without tenderness.

Balance is lost when children do not feel your love along with your correction.

We must continually show our children affection. I kissed my mother and father goodnight every day until I left for college. My children know that in the morning I become quite upset if they walk out of the house and don't kiss me. When I take them to school, I lay hands on them and pray, "Father, cover them, rebuke evil, and protect them from harm." We need to take the time to touch our children properly. Even if you didn't grow up that way, God will give you the ability to do it.

*So I will restore to you the years that the swarming locust has eaten* (Joel 2:25).

God will restore everything that the enemy took from you through either your parents' mistakes or your own. Claim it for your family! He will put into you what you are supposed to have to meet the needs of your children. You can learn a new way to parent and truly make this the beginning of a new, victorious generation.

The children need to see that you are tender with your spouse, too. It should be normal for you to kiss your husband or wife when you leave or return home. It's a wonderful thing for children to see their parents in love. Smile at your babies together. They will respond more easily to you and make you feel like you light up a room whenever you enter it.

If we have not forgiven our parents for the past, we will walk around angry and give birth to children who are angry, although they will not know the reason for it. Our children will become depressed if we act that way ourselves. Our society is filled with a generation of angry and resentful children. Don't provoke them to anger because of your lack of love or emotion or presence in their lives. Don't provoke them by being too busy. Love them unconditionally and pay attention to them every day.

At night, I ask my daughters to hug and kiss their mother and I before they go to bed. And I lay my hand on their foreheads and bless them in the name of the Lord before they go to sleep. I see this is a part of responsible fatherhood.

## Unconditional Love

Some of us frown too much. Recently, I went to a fast food restaurant, and the girl who was waiting on me didn't smile at all. I told her, "You're too young not to smile." In far too many cases, young girls like this one have been emotionally bruised at a young age by an absent or abusive father, grandfather or uncle. By the time I came to the store for a hamburger, she felt forsaken by all men, and I just happened to represent them. So she could not bring herself to smile at me. How sad that is. She will always have a difficult time relating to men unless she begins to seek God for the power to overcome her past.

Men often have a harder time showing tenderness than women, but our children need to experience love and tenderness from both their parents. We, as men, need to make a conscious effort to reach out to our children.

## Redemption for Families

We talked about the breakdown in family lives at the time of Malachi. Not only does God end the Old Testament with the words,

> *And he will turn the hearts of the fathers to the children, And the hearts of the children to their fathers...*(Malachi 4:6).

But He also says in the first chapter of Luke:

> *He will also go before Him in the spirit and power of Elijah, to turn the hearts of the fathers to the children, and the disobedient to the wisdom of the just, to make ready a people prepared for the Lord* (Luke 1:17).

It is as if God is trying to underline these thoughts for us because they are so important to Him.

It doesn't say that He will turn the minds or wills of

the fathers to the children—rather, it says He will turn *their hearts*. Although it may not come easy for us men, God will help us to provide the emotional support that our children need.

## Lap Time

Both your daughter and your son need tenderness. They need what I call "lap time." Have them sit down by you and let them know they are a blessing. Say things like, "From the moment God sent you, you have been a blessing to me. I just don't know what I'd do without you." It's unhealthy to correct our children and never console them. We need to bring our children close to us and let them feel our love and acceptance. Let them know that even though we may be disappointed by something they may have done, we are delighted because they're ours.

Every child needs love, attention, and care. Love your children unconditionally—all of them. Be sure your touch, your words, and your actions send the same important message to each one—that they are loved.

## Proud To Be a Father

I'm proud to be a father. I couldn't wait for my wife Phyllis to become pregnant. We really wanted to have children. We were only married three months when she conceived. It was a very exciting time, full of new life, possibilities, and promise.

It's an honor to be a father. You may lose your hair because of it, but it's an honor. Fathers, we are called to restore the sanctity of the family. One of the greatest things in life any man can do is choose the right wife and be a good father to his children. God help us to teach this to our boys!

Fathers, your daughters also need your touch. My daughters enjoyed me combing their hair when they were younger. Little girls sometimes go through stages where they only want "their daddy to do it." That loving safe, fatherly touch will build confidence in them. They may have the strength to wait for the man God has destined for them to marry just because you took the time to show them tenderness, care, and concern. God is calling fathers to nurture, cover, and protect their children.

I once heard a story about a young boy who was too scared to turn off his bedroom light one night.

His father said, "Boy, go to bed. Turn the light off. Don't be afraid of the dark. God is with you."

The boy responded, "I know He's with me, but I want somebody with some skin on them." This young boy wanted to identify with someone whom he could touch and feel. We put the "skin" on the principles and values of God for our children. We make them real to our children so that when they mature, they will be able to have a close relationship with God.

Lift your children up to God daily. Pray *for* them and

*with* them. Lay your hand on their heads as you pray. Tuck your children into bed as often as you can. Let their last sight of the day be of you bending over them with a kiss, wishing them a pleasant sleep.

During His earthly life, Jesus always had many people around Him who were seeking His ministry. It's significant that in the midst of all the miraculous activity, He gathered children onto His lap. Shouldn't we go and do likewise because our lap is a safe harbor for our children.

## HELPFUL HINTS

Don't assume that only the little ones need tenderness. Everyone, at every age, needs to be shown attention and tenderness. This can take many forms:

1. Thank them for something they have done that you really appreciate.

2. Express your love and appreciation for the wonderful person they are becoming.

3. Tell them how much you enjoy being with them.

4. Compliment them on the way they look.

5. Hug them first thing in the morning.

If you're not doing this type of thing on a regular basis, you are starving your family members and perhaps driving them to go elsewhere to find affection, attention, and appreciation. But when you consistently gather your family close to you, you build self-esteem without which no one can be successful.

*While we are doing
all we can to raise our
children properly, our children
may need to be loved in ways
that are not readily apparent
to us. Pause from the daily
routine of giving directives
and offering advice so that you
can listen to your children's
questions, fears, joys,
and sorrows.*

# Chapter VI

# Talk—Share It!

Before Nehemiah and the Israelites completed the gates to the wall of Jerusalem, Sanballat and Geshem, their enemies, tried to distract them from finishing the task. They sent word to Nehemiah to meet with them, but he refused. Instead, he...

> ...sent messengers to them with this reply: "I am carrying on a great project and cannot go down. Why should the work stop while I leave it and go down to you? But they sent me this message four times, and I answered them in the same manner." (Nehemiah 6:3-4)

Undaunted, they continued to try to frighten the Israelites, making up stories that the Israelites were preparing to rebel against the king.

*Then I sent to him, saying, "No such things as you say are being done, but you invent them in your own heart." For they all were trying to make us afraid, saying, "Their hands will be weakened in the work, and it will not be done."*

By simply talking with them, the enemies of the Israelites hoped to deter them from completing their God-given task.

Talk is powerful...words are mighty. God created the world and all that is in it by His very words.

*Then God said, "Let there be light"; and there was light* (Genesis 1:3).

The gospel of John opens with:

*In the beginning was the Word, and the Word was with God, and the Word was God* (John 1:1).

John not only says that Jesus *spoke* the word, but he also describes Him as *being* the Word. Jesus is God's communication with us. The new millennium is considered the Age of Communication. We are bombarded by words, both for good and for evil, from all sides—on radio, T.V., or on the Internet. Words have both the power to bless and the power to curse. Few memories are greater in the minds of children than the ones where Mommy or Daddy holds them and says, "Everything's going to be all right" or "Great job!" Our words as parents are much more powerful than we can imagine.

For example, after we have brought discipline into their lives, it is important that we make sure they understand it. But it is equally important that we also remind them of how much they mean to us and that this is the reason we won't let them get into foolishness. The Bible says that the fool walks in darkness, so we need to make it clear to them that we refuse to let them grow up to be fools.

## Speaking God's Word

We are called to be the most important influence in our children's lives. We must speak God's Word over them regularly. In our congregation, we invite the children to the altar for prayer several Sundays a year. We call it "The Children's Moment." We declare God's blessings over them and declare that Satan will not have his way in their lives. Many voices in our culture want our children for their selfish ends, but God gives us the authority to say, "No!" to them. At the same time, He gives us the power to say "Yes" to His promises for their blessings.

## An Everyday Thing

Teaching our children the ways of God can be done directly, through regular family Bible study; or indirectly, through the words we use in our everyday circumstances.

> *And these words which I command you today shall be in your heart. You shall teach them diligently to your children, and shall talk of them when you sit in your house, when you walk by the way, when you lie down, and when you rise up. You shall bind them as a sign on your hand, and they shall be as frontlets between your eyes. You shall write them on the doorposts of your house and on your gates* (Deuteronomy 6:6-9).

When you refrain from speaking badly about someone who has hurt you, your children will look at you and wonder why. When someone cuts you off in traffic and you respond with "Thank God there was no accident and bless that driver, Lord" you will say more about your principles and values than you could in a year's worth of Bible studies. Daily happenings are the perfect opportunity in which to share the principles you live by. It will mean so much more to them than a lesson from a book. They will have seen it lived out in front of them and then explained by the one whom they trust.

## Just for the Fun of It

Talking together can also be fun. Taking the time to share around the kitchen table, both during and after a meal, can draw you closer as a family. Some children will more easily join in than others. Be sure to make room for the quieter ones so they can participate too. In the give and take of the moment, you may be surprised at how much they will share.

When you go on vacation in a car, make sure that at least part of the time they remove their headphones and relate to one another. Find games to play along the way so that you're not each in your own world the entire time. A family vacation should be a celebration for the entire family to enjoy *together*.

## Listen As Much As You Speak

We as parents need to be silent long enough to listen to our children's words. While we are doing all we can to raise our children properly, our children may need to be loved in ways that are not readily apparent to us. Pause from the daily routine of giving directives and offering advice so that you can listen to your children's questions, fears, joys, and sorrow.

Our children are being surrounded by dangerous problems and situations. Kids are coming to school with guns, and they're shooting other children and teachers out of revenge. It's happening all across this country. (In my first book, *Stop the Funeral*, I speak more directly and at length about these issues. *Safe Harbor* is a book about solutions to those problems.) We need to help our children share their fears with us so that we can minister God's Word of protection and peace to them. We need to have an open line of communication with them, so that if there is some potential danger, we can deal with it appropriately.

## Children Need to Listen, Too

We also need to teach them to listen. The young boy Samuel was aroused from his sleep in the temple by a voice calling his name in the middle of the night. Samuel thought that Eli the priest was calling, so he went to him. But Eli responded, "I didn't call you. Go back to bed."

The voice came again: "Samuel, Samuel." So Samuel went to Eli again, but this time Eli told him that it probably was the Lord speaking to him. "The next time you hear the voice," Eli told him, "say 'Speak, Lord, Thy servant is listening.'" So Samuel went back to bed, and the third time he heard the voice, he asked the Lord to speak. (See 1 Samuel 3.)

If we'll quiet ourselves before Him, He will speak. He will speak to the dark, dry places in our lives, our homes, and our families, and renew our purpose and promise. We also need to teach our children to listen for God's voice, as Samuel did. They need to hear His voice louder than they hear the ones that are beckoning them toward evil. Our children will be faced with forces that are stronger than they are. We must teach them to speak with the power that is in the Name above all names and to listen for His direction for their lives. When they do, they will be resting in the safe harbor of home.

---

### HELPFUL HINTS

Do you know what is important to each of your family members? Do you know what areas of concern or fears they may have or what dreams and goals they cherish? If you want to know what makes them tick, there's only one way to find out—listen to them carefully. Ask them questions. If they have trouble sharing with you, then tell them something about yourself that they may not know—perhaps some lesson you learned through a difficult experience or a dream that you have. Openness with others often helps to "break the ice."

*Build the walls
of good memories around
your children so tall that they
cannot climb over them.
Make them walls of peace
and joy. Celebrate with
your children as the
Israelites regularly
did in their
feasts.*

## Chapter VII

# Tradition—Make It!

After the gates were completed to the walls of Jerusalem, and the people were settled in their houses, Ezra brought the Law before the assembly and read it aloud while the people listened attentively.

The people began to weep from conviction when they heard the Words of the Law, but Nehemiah said,

*And Nehemiah, who was the governor, Ezra the priest and scribe, and the Levites who taught the people said to all the people, "This day is holy to the LORD your God; do not mourn nor*

*weep." For all the people wept, when they heard the words of the Law. Then he said to them, "Go your way, eat the fat, drink the sweet, and send portions to those for whom nothing is prepared; for this day is holy to our LORD. Do not sorrow, for the joy of the LORD is your strength"* (Nehemiah 8:9-11).

When Ezra read that the Israelites were to live in booths during the feast of the seventh month, all the people went out and once again began the tradition that symbolized so much for the Israelites. In Leviticus 23:43, they were instructed to live in booths for seven days each year in remembrance and celebration of when the Lord brought them out of Egypt.

Again, when the Israelites crossed over into the Promised Land, God wanted to make sure they would never forget what He had done. He instructed them,

*Cross over before the ark of the LORD your God into the midst of the Jordan, and each one of you take up a stone on his shoulder, according to the number of the tribes of the children of Israel, that this may be a sign among you when your children ask in time to come, saying, "What do these stones mean to you?" Then you shall answer them that the waters of the Jordan were cut off before the ark of the covenant of the*

*LORD; when it crossed over the Jordan, the wa-
ters of the Jordan were cut off. And these stones
shall be for a memorial to the children of Israel
forever* (Joshua 4:5-7).

God knew the importance of tradition, especially in
the lives of young ones. Throughout the centuries, He
continually had the Israelites build memorials at places
where something significant happened. Tradition not
only builds memories but also continuity with the past.

## Family Traditions

Tradition. Do you remember the traditions your
family observed when you were growing up? I will never
forget Sunday dinners. In my youth, Sunday was special.
Many mothers cooked a huge meal on Saturday in
preparation for the rest and celebration that accompa-
nies Sunday. My mother wouldn't wash clothes or iron
on Sunday because it was the Lord's day. When we came
home from church, dinner was ready. This was a
common experience for many. Church worship was followed by a wonderful meal of roast beef and gravy, potatoes, hot biscuits, corn, and sweet potato pie calling to
us to the table. For us, Sunday was "dining room" day.
We rarely entered the dining room during the week, but
on Sundays, that was the place to be.

Today, you may not have a dining room, but that's

not the issue. Start some traditions for your family that they will always look forward to and cherish. There should be a "special season" when the "good dishes" are used. The dishes are not the issue, though, being together and making a special moment is. And that special moment can even be acknowledged with paper plates and plastic forks, as long as we do it together. Do something to build the walls of good memories so tall around your children that they cannot climb over them. Make them walls of peace and joy. Celebrate with your children as the Israelites regularly did in their feasts. An easy way to start is by celebrating the feasts of the church. But make each of your celebrations unique to your family. As you join together in devising these traditions, don't be surprised at seeing big smiles and shining eyes on your children. Children love traditions. And when the next year rolls around, you won't have to remind them about the celebrations, they will probably have been thinking about them for weeks.

What kind of traditions do you already have? You may have begun some that you can emphasize in a greater way. Above all, do your children ever feel that their lives are celebrated, and that they are special? If so, when do they experience those joys? For example, do you take them out for ice cream just to celebrate a minor milestone in their lives? If they receive a good report card, do you make it a tradition to take them someplace special? If they performed in a play at school, do you take the entire family out for dessert afterwards to make the experience a memorable one?

It doesn't matter how much or how little the celebration costs—a trip to the park that costs nothing can be just as memorable for them as a fancy dessert or a ride on a roller coaster. What they desire deep down is time shared with you. And remember, they don't always have to accomplish something to earn special attention, so do some things for them "just because you love them."

## Time Is Precious

Recently, one of the women in our church was diagnosed with breast cancer, and unfortunately, it has spread everywhere. As I took her frail hands in mine and knelt by her side, she told me, "I'm not ready to leave, Bishop. My children..." When you see people like that, who ache to have more time left to be with their children, it puts things into perspective. How many games of ball have you played with your children? How many times did you take them to McDonald's for breakfast? Do you support them in their schoolwork by providing extra help if they are struggling? Have you ever spent special one-on-one time out with each of them?

If you were to leave this world in the near future, like that young mother, do your children have a close enough relationship with God to be able to stand on their own? Do they know enough about His ways to know the difference between right and wrong, good and evil, light and darkness? Do they have discernment? Do they know enough about the Word of God and the deception of the enemy that they will not be tossed about by every wind of doctrine?

It's not just our responsibility to put food on the table and clothes on the children's backs, it's also our responsibility to transfer a tradition of faith and holiness to them. Our children desperately need to have an understanding of who God is. Family time, when you discuss some Scriptures or share what God has done in the lives of family or church members, will increase their faith. Prayer time is especially important because they will begin to see God move in response to their prayers. Little by little, they will develop a tradition of praying to Him on their own. Encourage them to seek Him. As they grow older, they will need to understand God in new ways that will help them deal with the world they will be entering.

Our traditions help hold them fast to God when everything around them may be flying around in the wind. Our traditions will help us build the safe harbor that our family needs.

## HELPFUL HINTS

What events bring back fond memories for you? More importantly, are you now building fond memories in your kids' lives? Are holidays a time of joy or stress? Do holidays and celebrations drive your kids away or anchor them firmly into your growing family traditions?

Things necessary to build traditions:
1. The time should be joy-filled not stressful.
2. The event is something that can be repeated year after year.
3. The event should be appropriate for the ages of the children—it can be modified from time to time to better fit them.
4. Take pictures and put them in an album that you can look at and talk about throughout the year.
5. Let the children help you plan them.

*Transitioning children for their adult life is not always easy. We have to be careful not to cut them loose before the proper time. But when they are ready, they can sail out with their own anchor on board—their relationship with the Lord— which will hold them steady despite the weather.*

## Chapter VIII

# Transition—Teach It!

T he dedication of the wall that Nehemiah and the Israelites built was a time of celebration. It was also a time when men were appointed to take their proper places in the community of the Israelites.

*Now at the dedication of the wall of Jerusalem they sought out the Levites in all their places, to bring them to Jerusalem to celebrate the dedication with gladness, both with thanksgivings and singing, with cymbals and stringed instruments and harps (Nehemiah 12:27).*

*And at the same time some were appointed over the rooms of the storehouse for the offerings, the firstfruits, and the tithes...Both the singers and the gatekeepers kept the charge of their God and the charge of the purification* (Nehemiah 12:44-47).

*And I appointed as treasurers over the storehouse...for they were considered faithful* (Nehemiah 13:13).

Whether they were gatekeepers, singers, or treasurers, God had given Nehemiah a place for each one. Today, we do a disservice to our children if we continue to support them after they become adults and don't help them discover their place. We are hurting them in the long run if we provide relief for their circumstances instead of demanding responsibility from them. We are holding them captive and not letting them become mature enough to live on their own. We are, in effect, crippling our children.

## A Place From Which They Can Sail

A safe harbor is not only a refuge from the storms of life, but it is also a good place from which to sail. Dangerous harbors can cause accidents and sinkings before the boats ever reach the sea. But from a safe harbor, our children can sail out onto the waters of life without worry about capsizing before they arrive. If they sail out from a secure place, they are relaxed and ready for the storms that will eventually come. If our training has created order in their lives, they can launch out without fear. They will not cut off their lines of communication to the harbor so if they get into trouble out there, they can always call home and talk with those who have been out on the seas before, and who know how to navigate the storms.

Transitioning children into their adult life is not always easy. Sometimes they want to do it before they are ready, and we have to be careful not to cut them loose before the proper time. But when they are ready, they can sail out with their own anchor on board—their relationship with the Lord—which will hold them steady, despite the weather.

## Preparation

Just as the people in Nehemiah's time were appointed to take positions because of their character and giftings, so too will our children take their places in life. If we have developed character in them, if we have thoroughly trained them in the way they should go, when they are old they will not depart from it. If they are prepared, their gifts will make a place for them, and they can be mightily used by God.

*When I was a child, I spoke as a child, I under-*
*stood as a child, I thought as a child; but when I*
*became a man, I put away childish things*
(1 Cointhians 13:11).

Yes, there comes a time when your children will
have to put away childish things. Have you prepared
them for it? Have you helped them learn self-discipline
so that they don't need someone constantly watching
over their shoulders to make sure that something gets
done? Have they come to a place of maturity because
you consistently demanded integrity and responsibility
from them? Are they prepared to take their place and
build on the wall? Are they trained to be appointed by
the leaders in their community to contribute to the body
as a whole? Are they prepared to construct a safe harbor
for their own families?

If so, God will say to us,

*Well done, good and faithful servant; you were*
*faithful over a few things, I will make you ruler*
*over many things. Enter into the joy of your lord*
(Matthew 25:21).

## HELPFUL HINTS

Are your children ready to sail off on their own? Here's some practical things you can do to help them make the transition:

1. Let them know that you're always ready to listen if they need to talk.

2. Give them room to make mistakes in matters that are not critical. As they begin to make wise choices and show a good measure of self-discipline, gradually let them have more control over their lives.

3. Support them in their decisions (as long as it doesn't put them in danger)...stand by them... and NEVER say "I told you so!" Let them come to appreciate your wisdom on their own.

*It is the responsibility
of the church to bring structure,
direction, guidance, and covering
to the unprotected ones of the
next generation. If there are
unfathered children in a
church, it becomes the
responsibility of every man
in the church to provide
a positive role model
for them.*

# Chapter IX

# Build the Walls Together!

Some of the children in our churches are not experiencing the family life that we have been talking about in this book. Perhaps they have a father who is in jail, or perhaps their mother was never taught responsibility, and she doesn't know how to raise them. It is difficult to model something right when all you have is something that is wrong .

As the church, we are called to a ministry of caring, consoling, and correcting with the mercy and love of Jesus. We are called to take bold action and reach out and touch those who are searching for a better way. We are called to touch those parents who have no idea how to raise their children. Every church should have some type of parenting classes to help them. We are called to touch those children whose lives are bruised and broken. If you walked into some neighborhoods, you would see valleys filled with tenements, homeless people lining the streets, young children with bulging eyes out at all hours of the night, and emaciated teenagers waiting for their next fix. The church today should be a safe harbor for these people and help them rebuild the walls of their own families. We are not to run and hide; rather, we are compelled by God's love to get into the trenches of life and make a difference. We are called to be salt—to make life once more appealing to these people; and light—to show the way to a different kind of life.

## Standing in the Gap

The church should stand in the gap and help rebuild the walls of these children's lives. These are not abstract ideas. Our God is a practical God; He desires that we give feet to our principles, and wings to our promises. For example, if your family is going on vacation, why not bring along another child or two who could benefit from the experience? Do you see a child hanging around the edges of some of the children's groups at church? Invite them home with you and reach out to them. If they do not experience family at all, how will they become ma-

74

ture? Unless God miraculously intervenes, their lives will perpetuate the madness that their parents forced on them. A boy can only learn how to be a man by watching another man. If you are a single mother, find a holy, godly man who will be an example for your boy to follow. You need to demand that your sons contribute to family life as well as your daughters. You won't help your son if you make him think that helping keep things clean is beneath him. My father was courageous in his confrontations. He meant what he said, and I was expected to follow the rules he set down. As such he was able to make me into a man who learned to obey authority and show respect. Because he did that, no policeman ever had to.

Parenting is about sacrifice. Contemporary rap artist, LL Cool J says, "All I ever wanted was a father." How many young people today does he represent? How do we, as a church, insulate our children from being damaged by fathers who won't bother or mothers who are so self-absorbed in their own psychotic past that they have no emotional connections with their children? If a mother and father do not mark their children for God, it is a responsibility of the church to step into the gap and supplement the children's teaching.

For the adults, every relevant church must have teaching and understanding on how to become a good parent. This teaching should include an understanding of how Hannah marked her son Samuel for service to the Lord. It should confront us with the question, "What is it that we want to mark our son or daughter for?" We mark them to fulfill the promise and experience the prosperity for which they were born. As the authority in our homes, we have to cut off wickedness and declare godliness, holiness, and integrity. For those children who have no one to do that for them, the church must take up the slack.

It is the responsibility of the church to bring structure, direction, guidance, and covering to the uncovered and unprotected ones of the next generation. If there are unfathered children in a church, it becomes the responsibility of every man in the church to provide positive role models for them. We are all busy. It is far better for us to make the sacrifices *now*, to take the time *now*, to make an investment in a child *now*. Or we will suffer the consequences later. Far too often those consequences involve jail time, unemployment, poverty and a repetition of a cycle of negativity.

The angel woke Joseph up to warn him about the danger that Jesus was in:

> *Now when they had departed, behold, an angel of the Lord appeared to Joseph in a dream, saying, "Arise, take the young Child and His mother, flee to Egypt, and stay there until I bring you word; for Herod will seek the young Child to destroy Him." When he arose, he took the young*

*Child and His mother by night and departed for Egypt* (Matthew 2:14)

Jesus was Joseph's son by adoption, but Joseph had a responsibility to protect Him. We need to reach out to the sons and daughters in our churches who have no parents protecting them. We need to show them the principle of hard work and find ways in which to train them for jobs. We need to warn those daughters about men who would take advantage of them. We need to expose the ways of the enemy to them.

We never know whose life God is calling us to intersect. We are called to reach beyond ourselves and our immediate family and start reaching out to other children who might need us. Perhaps God gave you that recent raise in your paycheck to help one of these little ones.

I believe the church has a real message of truth and renewal for a corrupt world. The church is our last chance.; if the church does not help stem the tide of unparented children, violence, and parental irresponsibility, it will not happen. We're the remaining message of hope and deliverance for the world.

When we know the Lord as the source of all we ever need, we will cross the paths of those around us with love, power, care, and compassion in our hearts. We will have the answer to our community's thirst for crack cocaine, heroin, and weed. He will give us creative solutions for teenage pregnancy and joblessness. The church and community are called to work together and find solutions.

We need to move beyond dressing up and looking the part of a Christian on Sundays. The time for playing church is over. When folks come into the church, they come to be a part of its ministry. They are coming to be embraced by God's people. They need generous servings of purity, holiness, and love, along with large helpings of care and compassion. They're looking for something different. They're looking for people who can help them, not tear them down. The church is the last hope for so many in the next generation. We need more than a form of religion. We need a vibrant, living faith that is both relevant and responsible. We are called to a real relationship with the people God has created.

## Becoming Prepared

In order to meet the myriad of needs in our communities, we must hide the Word of God deep within our hearts, as it is written in Psalms 119:11-16.

*Your word I have hidden in my heart, That I might not sin against You! Blessed are You, O LORD! Teach me Your statutes! With my lips I have declared All the judgments of Your mouth. I have rejoiced in the way of Your testimonies,*

*As much as in all riches. I will meditate on Your precepts, And contemplate Your ways. I will delight myself in Your statutes; I will not forget Your word.*

These words are the creed of a faithful follower who daily seeks the Lord. We are to obey the Lord's commands and prompting. Those who follow Him find fulfillment as they walk in His steps and reach out to the hurting ones around them. If we only follow the Lord when it's convenient, we experience discontentment, which eventually hardens into apathy.

Apathetic people rarely care about the state of the world or even their own community. They just sit idly by and say, "Whatever." In other words, "whatever the devil wants to do in my life is all right by me. Whatever happens in the community is all right too. Whatever happens is what happens, that's all." Then, of course, there is that part of the church who is so heavenly centered that they are oblivious to societal concerns. In Acts chapter 3, we read of Peter and John enroute to prayer. They paused and looked at a lame beggar—lifted him by the right hand and restored him to the community. We are called to prayer and practice, love and lifting.

Quite frankly, I am tired of the church saying, "Whatever." We should be concerned about the state of things. Wherever there is pain, the Church needs not only to show up but to also find creative ways in which to help.

When we learn to rest in God and trust Him, He will lead us to minister. He will move through us to confront the problems in our homes, down the street, and in our churches.

I heard a story at a ministerial convention that helps to illustrate this point. The story concerned an Arab shepherd in the Middle East. One day, as a Christian group was touring Israel, a shepherd told some ministers, "Your Jesus spoke of sheep and shepherds. I, Shepherd Abdul, know every one of my sheep by name. When I call, they come."

So the preachers pointed to a sheep nearby and challenged him, "Abdul, call that sheep here."

Abdul responded, "Give me two dollars."

"What do you mean, give you two dollars? Is this some sort of game?" the skeptical ministers asked.

"I need two dollars so I can go buy some oats," Abdul explained. "When I put the oats in my hand and call their names, the sheep come to eat the oats. No oats, no sheep."

The point of this story is that the sheep respond to the presence of the food. We must make sure that we present the real food of life when we try and minister, instead of empty promises and meaningless slogans.

When we, ourselves, consistently partake of the bread of life, then we have something to offer people who are searching for a safe harbor for themselves and their families.

## The Responsible Church

In order to snatch some of these lost ones from the stormy seas of life and bring them into a safe harbor, we need to seek to meet both their physical and spiritual needs.

> *If a brother or sister is naked and destitute of daily food, and one of you says to them, "Depart in peace, be warmed and filled," but you do not give them the things which are needed for the body, what does it profit? Thus also faith by itself, if it does not have works, is dead. But someone will say, "You have faith, and I have works. Show me your faith without your works, and I will show you my faith by my works"* (James 2:15-18).

We have become a very self-centered, self-obsessed people. We forget too quickly how someone helped us when we were going through hard times. Someone cared enough to give us a spare car, a refrigerator, or a job when we needed them. This is relevant Christianity. Some people have two cars but won't volunteer to pick up a singe mother with three children and bring them to church. They see the woman walking with her children to the bus stop in the rain and drive right on by.

Most of us would be surprised at how much we have accumulated around the house that could prove to be a real blessing to people. People plan garage sales that won't earn them more than $15 or so. They could spare themselves the trouble and give the old cabinet or dishes to some struggling parent.

I'm talking about being responsible Christians. When you know your neighbor's husband suffered a stroke and is incapacitated, who do you think God wants to use to help that wife? Responsible Christians see the need and move to meet it.

"Mother Brown, has anyone been to your house to shovel the snow?"

"No, Baby."

"Mother Brown, I'll be right over."

"Baby, I ain't got nothin' to pay you with, but I made some fried chicken yesterday. And you take your wife Ernestine a piece of this cake."

"If you say so, Mother."

Now that is real Christianity at work. God uses people—everyday, ordinary people—who love God enough to want to make a difference. The Scripture says in 1 John 3:14, "We know that we have passed from death to life, because we love the brethren."

People with children, especially teenagers, can begin

to put this kind of Christian responsibility into their lives today. You can point out someone's need as being an opportunity for them to begin to minister to others. Then put the tools in their hands and step back.

Let's be the responsible Church, allowing Him to position us and use us to help create the safe harbors that others so desperately need.

*Let your light so shine before all people, that they may see your good works and glorify your Father in heaven* (Matthew 5:16).

The responsible Church says, "The Lord is my shepherd, guide, and director. The Lord leads me, *not* the past. The Lord leads me, not anger. The Lord leads me, *not* competition. The Lord leads me, *not* revenge. "

The responsible Church reaches out and looks at Chavelle in the eye and says, "How are you doing this morning, Sister? You know that child looks just like you. I want to buy him some milk. Will you let me?"

"How are you this morning, young man? Is your Daddy still out? Ask your mother if you can spend the afternoon with my two sons and me today. We're going to a ballgame. Let me see if your mother will have supper with us. If she's busy, maybe you can come by yourself."

"How are you this morning, Brother? You need any help around your place this week? Oh, you're painting? Need any help? I whip a mean brush!"

This is how saints in the responsible church are supposed to live.

*Then the King will say to those on His right hand, "Come, you blessed of My Father, inherit the kingdom prepared for you from the foundation of the world: for I was hungry and you gave Me food; I was thirsty and you gave Me drink; I was a stranger and you took Me in; I was naked and you clothed Me; I was sick and you visited Me; I was in prison and you came to Me."*

*Then the righteous will answer Him, saying, "Lord, when did we see You hungry and feed You, or thirsty and give You drink? When did we see You a stranger and take You in, or naked and clothe You? Or when did we see You sick, or in prison, and come to You?"*

*And the King will answer and say to them, "Assuredly, I say to you, inasmuch as you did it to one of the least of these My brethren, you did it to Me"* (Matthew 25:34-40).

We should be genuinely concerned for the weary, scattered, stressed-out masses around us. They include the brokenhearted, the single parent with five babies, the teenagers who have just had abortions, the unemployed, uneducated, and improperly parented. They are also people in position and power who look like they have it all, but who are devoid of peace and joy in their souls. If we look closely, we will see that they, too, are broken, shallow, and hurting. They, too, need the healing touch of the Savior's hand. They, too, need a safe harbor in which to dwell.

God desires to raise us up not only to create a safe harbor for our families, but also to reach out to our communities and draw other families into the same place of peace, safety, and purpose. Let us send out the beacon of light from our homes that will dispel the darkness around us and together enlarge our harbors to bring hope, joy, and peace to the communities in which we live!

## Safe Harbor Begins @Home

I was hungry
  and you formed a humanities club
  and you discuss my hunger.
  Thank you.
I was imprisoned
  and you crept off quietly
  to your chapel in the cellar
  to pray for my release.
I was naked
  and in your mind
  you debated the morality of my
  appearance.
I was sick
  and you knelt and thanked God
  for your health.
I was homeless
  and you preached to me
  of the spiritual shelter of the
  love of God.
I was lonely
  and you left me alone
  to pray for me.
You seem so holy
  so close to God.
But I'm still very hungry
  and lonely
  and cold.
So where have your prayers gone?
  What have they done?
  What does it profit a man to page through his
  book of prayers when the rest of the world is
  crying for help?
      —M. Lunn

# Other books from Evergreen Press by Dr. Donald Hilliard, Jr.

*Somebody Say Yes!*
Answers to the most pressing issues of the new millennium. Is success within our reach—are we ready for it? Is holiness within our hearts—can we embrace it? Is the family within our priorities—will we nurture it? Seventeen chapters that will encourage and challenge you to grow.
ISBN 1-58169-062-2  160 pp. hardcover $19.99

*How Daddy Can Make a Difference*
Shows fathers how to restore their families by providing attention, protection, nurture, and training for their kids.
ISBN 1-58169-071-1  16 pp. PB $1.99

*Handling Life's Pressure Situations*
How to victoriously deal with the pressures of life in today's complex world.
ISBN 1-58169-077-1  16 pp. PB $1.99

*Dealing With Delilah*
How to handle the temptation of forbidden pleasures and find true restoration.
ISBN 1-58169-079-7 16 pp. PB $1.99

# ABOUT THE AUTHOR

Bishop Donald Hilliard, Jr. recently celebrated 25 years of vital ministry to the church and community he serves. His mission is to evangelize, educate, emancipate, and empower individuals and families so they can realize their full potential. Dr. Hilliard's ministry is distinguished by cutting-edge leadership with a strong emphasis on faith, family, finances, and community development.

Dr. Hilliard is a graduate of Eastern College, St. Davids, PA (BA); Princeton Theological Seminary, Princeton, NJ (MDiv); and the United Theological Seminary, Dayton, OH (DMin). He was ordained to the Gospel ministry in 1976 and consecrated a bishop in 1995.

He is the Senior Pastor of The Cathedral, Second Baptist Church in Perth Amboy, NJ with over 5000 members, three locations, and nine properties. The Cathedral is known throughout the country for revitalizing the inner city and thereby making a significant impact on the people they serve.

Dr. Hilliard is the Presiding Bishop of Covenant Ecumenical Fellowship and Cathedral Assemblies. He is also a visiting professor of Church Renewal at Drew University School of Theology.

# FOR MORE INFORMATION

For more information about Dr. Donald Hilliard Jr.'s ministry or for speaking engagements, write or call:

The Cathedral • Second Baptist Church
277 Madison Ave. • P.O. Box 1608
Perth Amboy, NJ 08862
(732) 826-5293 ext. 1161
website: www.thecathedral.org
email address: bishop@thecathedral.org